NINE MONTHS

THE STORY OF WILBUR

TANIA TOMYN

authorHOUSE

AuthorHouse™
1663 Liberty Drive
Bloomington, IN 47403
www.authorhouse.com
Phone: 833-262-8899

© 2022 Tania Tomyn. All rights reserved.

No part of this book may be reproduced, stored in a retrieval system, or transmitted by any means without the written permission of the author.

Published by AuthorHouse 12/29/2022

ISBN: 978-1-6655-7902-5 (sc)
ISBN: 978-1-6655-7901-8 (e)

Library of Congress Control Number: 2022923792

Print information available on the last page.

Any people depicted in stock imagery provided by Getty Images are models, and such images are being used for illustrative purposes only. Certain stock imagery © Getty Images.

This book is printed on acid-free paper.

Because of the dynamic nature of the Internet, any web addresses or links contained in this book may have changed since publication and may no longer be valid. The views expressed in this work are solely those of the author and do not necessarily reflect the views of the publisher, and the publisher hereby disclaims any responsibility for them.

In memory of Willy, our sweet little angel
who blessed our lives and changed our world
far more than we ever thought possible.

May your tail wag each and every day
until we meet again.

Contents

Preface ix

1. June 1
2. July 9
3. August 15
4. September 17
5. October 19
6. November 21
7. December 24
8. January 27
9. February 29
10. March 31

Afterword 35
In Loving Memory of Flash 37
In Loving Memory of Wylie 39
Acknowledgments 43

Preface

This story was truly a labor of love. I first knew I needed to share our story of Wilbur twelve years ago. I started writing, and then I just couldn't. I stopped after the December chapter, and you will see why. It took me until I was forty-seven years old and had adopted four more "babies" (rescue pups), owned and closed three companies, gone through fertility issues, quit smoking, survived some heart issues, and moved eleven times, to complete the story of my nine months. Nine months with my baby, filled with mostly love and therefore pain and excruciating heartbreak.

I am lucky, yes lucky, that then and now I have had a strong partner and love of my life to stand by me and with me always. When you run businesses, lose businesses, move around the country (including to St. Croix, US Virgin Islands), and take care of rescue dogs, it is not always easy to be able to give each other the necessary love.

Dogs supply unconditional love. Humans need to make the effort. I am so thankful my partner wants to make the effort each day while being the best—yes, the *best*—doggie daddy ever!

Thank you, Aaron.

June

It was a perfect summer day as I drove, anxiety-ridden, down my street with my friend Michelle keeping me company in the passenger's seat. I had lived there two years, so the sights were very familiar, but on that day the scenery around my home was much different. Starting a few houses down from mine, I saw a crowd of parked cars on either side of the street. When I spotted the company pickup truck, I knew what I was about to walk into. I turned to Michelle and said, "Tell me that he didn't do this. I hate surprises. Just promise me …"

I parked the car, grabbed all my shopping bags, closed the garage, and walked inside cautiously. The house was buzzing, and Michelle quickly stepped in front of me, yelling "Hello!"

Suddenly there was silence. I made a few more steps, reached the hallway, and there it was. "Surprise!"

Yes, my thirty-fourth birthday bash was a surprise, thanks to my husband, Aaron.

Family and friends from all over the country, along with coworkers and Hank, our adorable white and tan shih tzu whom we considered our son, had gathered for a Hawaii-themed luau party. Hank was even adorned with a lei in lavender and coral colors. The bar in our living and dining room area was decorated with palm leaves and balloons, with a bartender serving up mai tais and whatever else he could conjure up. It was quite beautiful, and for a moment I felt I was in Hawaii. For a moment—since we live in Las Vegas, I could only imagine.

Hank at my birthday luau party

Finally, all the guests left, and it was down to Aaron, Hank, Michelle, and her husband, Luke. Peace at last. And then it came, the announcement I was not at all prepared for. Michelle gave at me a look I knew all too well and said, "We're pregnant."

Silence. There it was. My dream became a nightmare.

Aaron and I had been trying to conceive for over two years. The idea of pregnancy and raising a child with my husband had been on my mind daily. It had been such a struggle for us not to be blessed with a baby. We visited fertility specialists and pondered adoption, but always hung on to the hope that we would just have a baby naturally, as so many do every day in this world. Yes, we even tried "the egg"—three women I knew who had problems getting pregnant had tried "the egg," and shazam! Prego! Well, it didn't work for us, but we are both fighters. We decided to keep our heads up, and if it was meant to be, things would happen.

And on June 20, something did happen. We adopted our "baby," and his name was Wilbur.

The first time we saw Wilbur's sad little eyes was in a picture my best friend, Becky, emailed us with a message.

> Doesn't he look like Hank's long-lost brother? I had to send this to you because he looks so much like Hankie. My friend runs a pet rescue, and this dog is available for adoption. He was found on the streets of Pasadena and his eye was all messed up. The rescue had to raise money so he could get eye surgery and I donated.

Becky had no idea (well, maybe a slight idea) about what would happen next. Aaron took one look at the photo on his BlackBerry as he was boarding a flight from who-knows-where, and the deal was done. Sold. We completed the online application, spoke with the foster family, and were approved. Then we were on our way to pick up our new addition from the park in West Hollywood, where the rescue sets up every Saturday.

Hank, Aaron, and I were so excited as we drove up to the park after four hours in the car. We leapt out of the vehicle, ran up the sidewalk, and spotted Becky, who of course had to be there to witness the adoption. Becky greeted us with hugs, and as we were all embracing, I saw him. It is a picture engraved in my mind that I will never forget. There was sweet little Wilbur, cone and all, skinny and timid in his foster mother's arms. The cone around his head looked like a big satellite dish wrapped around a twig.

"Do you want to hold him?" she asked as I approached.

"Yes, please," I replied.

I held him tightly and cradled him like the baby I had always wanted.

As we all smiled, laughed, and took photos, snorts could be heard coming from the bundle of joy in my arms. Little did we know that Wilbur had been named quite appropriately, and there were many more snorts in our future.

What surprised me most that June day was how loving Aaron was with Wilbur. My husband was such a guy's guy and very masculine, but when he held that little dog that day, something changed. I didn't know then that at that moment a bond was created that would never be broken.

And this is where the story begins.

Wilbur's adoption day

The first night with our new addition to the family was an interesting one—stressful to the max. Did I mention that Wilbur snorted? Well, at night, the cute snort developed into a loud snore. Not a little, twelve-pound-dog snore. This was more of a five-hundred-pound human snore through a PA system. At first I thought the cone amplified the sounds, but when we took it off, the snoring was just as loud. And it's not like you can just slap a Breathe Right strip on his tiny, squished-in nose. There were no easy solutions for this situation, which I was not at all prepared for. So Aaron and I brainstormed.

For our first attempt, we gated the workout room (intended to be a nursery at some point) off our bedroom and set up a crate with the door open, doggie toys, and a down comforter to create a cozy environment. The incessant barking and banging on the gate were possibly worse than the snoring, not to mention heartbreaking. My stress and level of anxiety were reaching maximum status, and it was almost 3:00 a.m. We had to wake up in a few hours for work and be able to function and run our business. We had to figure out another solution.

Frustrated and ready to scream at the top of my lungs, I shot up out of bed, picked up Wilbur, put him in his crate, and carried him across our house to the family room. I left a light on for him and briskly walked out of the room with tears streaming down my face. You could still hear his high-pitched barks, so I shut the double doors of our bedroom, turned to Aaron and Hank, and asked, "Did we make a mistake? I cannot handle this. What do we do?"

Aaron reached for my hand and assured me that we had made the right decision by bringing Wilbur into our loving home and that we would find a remedy. Maybe his snoring was the reason he was abandoned and left on the streets. We did a good thing in rescuing him, and there was no way, Aaron said, we would let him ever feel abandoned again. I accepted his words and then cried myself to sleep.

The next few nights were not much better. We repeated the same steps of trying to keep Wilbur in our bedroom so he could feel we were close. Aaron even bought him a $200 giant dog pillow bed that we put in the workout room, and I tried sleeping on it with him until he fell asleep. But every time I moved even one inch, he was wide awake. So back in the crate he went. However, no matter how quietly I stepped over the gate to return into my bed, his nose and paw were through the grates and the barking started.

By the third night, Wilbur was in a crate in the middle of our bedroom. That was the only way he didn't bark. But the snoring was as loud as ever. I was in disbelief at the sounds that could come out of such a small dog. He made musical arrangements with his snores that ranged in volume and pitch. But after night three, the sounds I heard were muffled—I started putting in earplugs. And by the end of the month, I was able to sleep through the night with my ears stuffed. Relief at last.

But unfortunately, Wilbur did not have relief yet. He was uncomfortable between his snores, which did not allow him to sleep well, and the red spots all over his belly itched him along with his paws, which he chewed on continuously. And let's not forget that he still wore his cone because his eye was not completely healed from surgery.

My days became consumed with appointments I needed to take Wilbur to. I took him to Hank's vet and visited Dr. Minor as soon as I could so we could start relieving him from all his itching. Wilbur was the perfect patient as the doctor checked his eyes and ears and inspected the red spots and sores. The only thing that Wilbur wanted no part of was having his temperature taken in his behind. He made that pretty clear, so the thermometer went under the arm.

Dr. Minor assured me that Wilbur was in the right home and that with lots of love and regular visits, we would get him back to "normal." We departed the vet with some vitamins, antibiotics, and cream for his sores.

A couple of days later, I took Wilbur to the eye specialist for a follow-up visit. He'd had a conjunctival graft surgery back in early June, for which the rescue we adopted from had raised money. Again, he was the perfect patient, just sitting there as the lights in the exam room went on and off and even when green goo was put in his eye. I was amazed because Hank, even as well behaved as he is, is always a wiggle-butt at vet appointments.

Wilbur got the high sign, and we were good to go. But there was one last question Aaron had instructed me to ask.

"When can I take the cone off him?" I asked as nicely as I could.

"Well, he is healing well, so you can take it off when he eats, of course, and then at night if he doesn't bother his eye or look like he is trying to scratch it."

That was all I needed to hear. I knew as soon as I conveyed this message to Aaron, the cone was off for good.

That night, Wilbur slept and snored coneless. He never put a paw near his eye that or any other night.

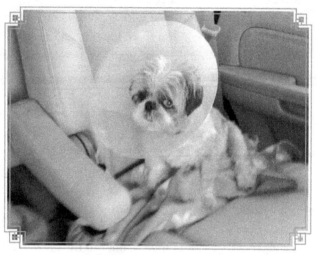

Baby Wilbur (Willy) with his cone

July

The snoring situation was still an issue, but it was tolerable—or at least we had learned to live with it. Hank no longer paced the bed with anxiety, Aaron now snored in harmony along with Wilbur, and I had my earplugs.

The employees at the office also became accustomed to the symphony of Wilbur. We had always brought Hank to the office, and so naturally Wilbur now came as well. Every morning, I packed the boys into the back seat of my sedan, which was covered by a down comforter they could snuggle in, and drove them to work with me. My husband and I have our own business, so we were fortunate enough to be able to have them with us all day. We had to mute our side on conference calls or roll Wilbur in his chair into another office if we had a client meeting, so the snoring would not disturb the business being conducted. But no matter what, everyone in the office could hear his snores. Luckily, everyone thought it was "cute," although I was asked repeatedly how I could sleep at night. I would take one look at Willy before stating, "Not always easy, but he's worth it."

He *was* worth it. Every bit. Wilbur gained popularity over Hank at the office. Hank is the perfect dog in so many ways, but Willy had something special – he touched your heart. He was sweet, of course, but he was so strong and loyal. If he were human, he would be one of those people you might never be fortunate enough to come across who never let you down and always fight with you, right at your side, until the very end. But he needed our help, and I believe this is what frustrated Wilbur the most. He wanted to give love, and he did, but he had health issues that caused him anxiety—he was helpless and needed us to help make him stronger.

I continued to take Wilbur to the vet. We tried everything we could to stop his itching, but he kept scratching himself. The sores got worse, and he would not stop chewing on his paws. The vet had given us a medicated shampoo to use, and we bathed him twice a week. The bath helped for a day, and then he would be miserable again. We hated that he was uncomfortable in any way. We thought maybe it was allergies, assuming Wilbur was not used to Las Vegas, so with Dr. Minor's recommendation, we started giving him half a Benadryl a day. Looking back, I think this made him more comfortable only because it made him drowsy and he could rest peacefully.

During one of our visits to the vet, it was discovered that Wilbur had an enlarged heart and slight murmur, so he was given two additional medications. The vet suggested that if I wanted a more accurate prognosis, I should take Willy to a cardiology specialist. So I made the appointment, and Aaron took the little guy for a cardiology consultation and ultrasound (echocardiogram). Six hundred dollars later,

Aaron was told that Willy had degenerative heart disease, a chronic degeneration of the valves on the left and right sides of the heart. The good news was that the condition did not seem advanced, and he would just need to be monitored. Recheck in six months. Noted.

What should also be noted is that Aaron at times tends to be a sucker. The cardiologist happened to hear Wilbur's snorts, Aaron mentioned the snoring dilemma, and it all went downhill from there. The doctor had talked Aaron into a procedure that would help Wilbur with his breathing by opening up his nostrils, and at the same time he would conduct a soft palate resection that would stop Willy from snoring. The specialist had seen this condition many times and assured that after the procedure, Wilbur's snore would be no more—or at the very least, be faint. This sounded great, but I was wary of putting Willy through any more "procedures." He had been poked and prodded persistently over the past few weeks. But if it would help him breathe easier, and allow his mom, dad, and Hank to sleep easier, maybe we would give it a shot. After all, what's another $1,200?

Dropping Wilbur off for his minor nose surgery was heartbreaking. Tears could not stop falling straight down my face as I handed him off to the nurse. What was more embarrassing was when I panicked. I ran out to my car to grab Willy's blankie and favorite little stuffed duck toy and brought them inside the doctor's office. The nurse said that bringing in these items probably did more to make me feel better than him, but they would make sure he received everything. I turned and stormed out in tears, fuming mad. How dare she speak to me like that when I was clearly upset and understandably irrational!

I was a wreck the rest of the day and all night. We missed Wilbur so much, and it was funny because we couldn't sleep without his snore! Morning could not come soon enough, as it meant I would be able to pick up our baby. I waited in an exam room for what felt like hours. Then finally, out came Willy, shiny new cone and all, looking so precious and in need of love. I scooped him up and held his limp little body in my arms and decided that he could stay cuddled in my lap for the ride home. He rested in my lap so peacefully as I drove, so silently, until … he started to snore.

I sure hope that the $1,200 we spent on the surgery helped Wilbur breathe better, because his snoring and snorting most definitely did not fade—instead it seemed louder than ever. Lesson learned.

At the end of the month, Wilbur's sores were doing a little better—not quite as red—and after nightly brushing the white flakes that used to fall from his body all over our bedspread seemed to lessen in quantity. We decided that he was finally ready for his first real grooming.

Aaron and I were so nervous about leaving Willy—as we had come to call Wilbur—in someone else's hands, even if it was only for a couple of hours. As we walked into the doggie day spa, Willy displayed the least fear of the three of us. He was happy to see the other dogs and social as usual. We told the ladies that he was special and we would pay extra for any extra care they needed to take. The list of instructions included being careful of his paws because they are very sensitive and they may not be able to clip his nails if it causes him any pain, his skin is sensitive so they need to use the special shampoo we brought, and do not scrub his belly as the sores there are very sensitive.

For the next two hours, I didn't let my cell phone leave my pocket, and I had the volume turned up as high as it would go so I could hear from the groomer when Willy was ready for pick-up. And when my phone finally rang three hours later, I made a twenty-minute drive in ten. As my sweaty hands opened the door of the shop, I was dying to see him and find out how he behaved. What a sight I saw! The most adorable shih tzu in the world greeted me, wearing a lime-green and multicolored-polka-dot bandana around his neck. He was white and tan, with his white parts standing out crisply after his cut and the perfect amount of fluff to him. The best part was that he was happy, and the report was even better. "Wilbur was a perfect gentleman. He did very well and was so patient," the owner told me.

Yes! "We are making progress," I told Willy on the drive back home to see his dad and brother. He turned to me and you could see how proud he was. He felt better knowing that he looked like a show dog; his whole demeanor changed.

When we arrived home, Willy was full of spunk and ran to his dad to show off his new "do." Hank had missed Willy and was so excited to see him that he ran up and tried to play and love on him, but Willy gave his brother a little nip and Hank backed right off. I wasn't sure whether he didn't want to get his hair messed up or just wasn't ready to play with Hank yet. But by bedtime, I caught the boys asleep on their blanket on our bed, with Willy's head resting gently on Hank's butt, cozy as can be. I immediately started snapping some photos because I wanted to capture their bond.

Wilbur, wearing his lime-green bandana from the groomer, resting on Hank for support

The four of us were becoming a family unit, and it was time for our first family trip.

August

Our first family trip was to the luxurious St. Regis Hotel in Dana Point, California. It took us a little over four hours to get there, and the boys were perfect angels in the back seat of Aaron's Escalade. They each had their own seat covered with a plush doggie bed and rested most of the way. Every hour or so, they stood up on their hind legs and peered out their respective windows to admire the scenery as it grew greener. Hank and Wilbur loved California.

As we drove up to valet at the hotel, you could feel the boys' excitement. They were so ready for their leashes and wanted to run around smelling and peeing on every bush, flower, and patch of grass. I was amazed at how aggressively Willy was smelling everything in sight. It was as if he was recognizing what he was breathing in. Maybe his nostril surgery had worked and the $1,200 was indeed well spent.

I had forgotten until then that Willy was originally found on the streets of Pasadena, about an hour and a half away, and wondered where exactly. Did he miss his old home? Did he have a brother or sister? Had he ever been loved and cared for?

Well, he was well cared for now, and he loved being pampered. Staying in our suite with doggie room service, plush beds, royalty-style water bowls, and gourmet treats pleased him. The more stars the hotel had, the better for him. And that was that: he was our North Star.

Aaron hanging with the boys at the St. Regis

September

September was a month full of visits to the doctor, as Wilbur's skin irritations were getting much worse. The medicated shampoo and ointments to ease his suffering were just not enough. We were searching for a miracle to help our little baby boy. He had already gone through so much that we didn't even know about, let alone his heart murmur and breathing issues. All we wished was for him to catch a break.

By the end of the month, Wilbur was gnawing on himself to a point where he needed to get a cast on his front paw, and then another and another. Pink tender-looking skin, itching until he bled from biting at it, was misery for him. The spaces between his toes were raw to a point where they were hard to look at. I knew it was painful and frustrating for him, and I felt so helpless.

Then I thought, *Could there be medications he was given previously that led to this?* My mind was racing. I knew that my own allergy to a drug caused me to break out in red and white hives and uncontrollable itching, with a high temperature.

I was told that I could die if I took the medication again. Could Wilbur be having a similar reaction? Did I miss something? *What do I do?*

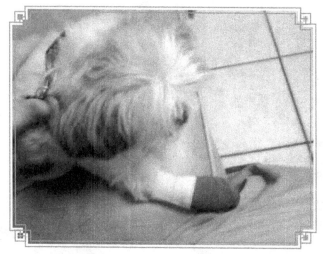

Willy getting his first cast on his front paw

October

October is always a favored month in our household, as we are big fans of Halloween. Dressing up and pretending to be whatever or whoever you want to be for the day? Come on! Scaring each other with wolf masks, fake blood, roaches, snakes, scorpions…. enough said.

It also became a tradition in our home to take our babies to a hotel for Halloween, so they don't have to deal with trick-or-treaters yelling and the constant knocking or ringing of a doorbell. Willy's first year we went to the Langham Hotel in Pasadena. Willy dressed up in a skeleton costume so he could feel like "skin and bones," and Hank regrettably had to wear a Red Wings jersey, since his mom was born and raised in Detroit and a huge hockey fan. He didn't love my choice for him, but patient as always, he reluctantly allowed me to put it on him and even take photos. After all, he was at the Langham, once again receiving doggie room service.

Pasadena is where we adopted Wilbur and where we believed he grew up, so we wondered if for a moment he felt a sense of peace and of being home. We later realized that the peace he felt came from wherever Aaron, Hank, and I were.

Hank and Wilbur in their Halloween outfits

November

November was devastating—definitely the most difficult month with Willy, because of the terrible news we received. His skin irritations just would not clear up no matter what cream or ointment we put on him and no matter how many medicated shampoo baths we gave him. Our vet was finally throwing in the towel and strongly recommended that I take Willy to a doggie dermatologist. I didn't even know that such a thing existed! After receiving the bill from the visit and almost falling flat on the floor, I decided that I was most definitely in the wrong line of work. Since most people treat their dogs like children and royalty, the doggie field was where I should be.

The dermatologist visit was interesting. I didn't feel very comfortable, and neither did Wilbur. The room we were put in was modern and cold. I understand that it was meant to be trendy, but it did not impress us. Wilbur and I snuggled and made the best of it until the "doctor" entered and began the consultation. After the initial examination of Willy's issues, I was asked if it was alright to take a few biopsies of the irritated red areas in question. Because I wanted some resolution to this never-ending saga, I agreed to put Willy through a minimal amount of discomfort now for the sake of answers and, I hoped, eventual eternal comfort.

What I did not know is that the decision to allow the biopsies was the best one I could have made for the rest of Wilbur's life. This appointment, exam, and almost one thousand dollars were worth more than I could have imagined when I reluctantly handed my credit card to the receptionist.

November also happens to be my husband's birthday month. So on the twelfth, Aaron's family and Hank and Wilbur were all there to celebrate. For a flash, we were a happy family. Then, just a few days later, we received Wilbur's results.

Aaron's mother, stepfather, and niece celebrating Aaron's birthday with us

What I learned in mid-November from the dermatologist—as I stared blankly at a computer screen, anxiety-ridden and trembling—was that his results showed cancer.

> This is not a cancer that responds well to chemotherapy and rarely goes into remission. Progression is unpredictable and may be rapid or slow over the next 14 months. Typically, this is a cancer that causes intense pruritus that is unresponsive to steroids. When it stops responding to steroids humane euthanasia must be considered.

And that was that. I slammed down the examination letter I had printed out. Time for something different.

December

December was the most eventful and spectacular month! Wilbur was doing so well with his chemo. No nausea or sickness at all. He was happy and full of life. As a family, we were all so excited for December 19 to arrive, because we had a road trip planned like no other we had taken.

Aaron likes to go overboard, so he rented an RV. But not just any RV: a forty-five-foot luxury RV with marble bathrooms and granite countertops in the kitchen. The RV rental would cost much more than we could afford, but Aaron reserved it anyway and put down the deposit without my knowledge—he knew if I had anything to do with it, we would be in a rickety old thirty-footer, but he wanted to ride in the lap of luxury with Willy.

We invited John, who worked with us, and his spouse and two children. So yes, we were going to drive across the country from Las Vegas to Detroit, Michigan, in an RV for four days with four adults, two dogs, and two children.

Everyone at work told us we were nuts and would never survive the trip. If they only knew!

The gigantic brown RV with khaki designs arrived at our home on December 18, and it was beautiful! I was so excited that I ended up packing it throughout the night so we would be ready to begin our venture early in the morning. I was interrupted, however, when Aaron had to show off the "bus" to our friends and workplace. We took a drive to our office and set up camp in the parking lot for a bit, inviting everyone we saw on board for a drink. As I sat on the plush leather couch, sipping my glass of wine, with ten of us on the parked RV, I knew right then we were going to have the trip of a lifetime.

How do I describe Wilbur on the RV trip? He was like a little old man who would not allow anyone else to take *his* copilot seat. He could not leave his dad's side while he was driving. Willy was this warm old soul, except for getting cold very easily due to his chemo treatments. We kept him in blankets constantly and even got him little booties to help keep his paws warm.

Willy in the copilot seat on the RV

Willy did play and enjoy his time with Mae and Johnny, John's children, and cuddled with his brother Hank on breaks from his duty as copilot. Wilbur even slept with little Mae a couple of nights on the RV. He had an instinct to love and care for this beautiful, innocent child. Now, if I strolled up front and tried to slide in and share the copilot seat, he would snort and snap at me!

There were so many good memories from this trip, but one that stands out as especially amusing was how interested Wilbur was in the snow in Colorado. He wanted to see it so badly when we stopped in Beavercreek to get coffee. He went and walked in the snow, probably never having seen it before, but then quickly begged for Aaron to pick him up because it was too cold. He had his taste and just wanted to feel warm arms of love again.

January

Our December trip came to an end in early January, and we were still on our high and exhilarated. How awesome it was to share Wilbur with our family and friends in Michigan. It felt so fulfilling to know that he got to share every moment of the holiday season with us. Wilbur even got to visit Aaron's family farm, all while remaining in the arms of his daddy. He was not enthralled with the cockatoo at Grandpa Smith's farmhouse, but what is Wilbur without a growl or two?

Then suddenly reality decided to slam us over the head like a glass bottle in a bar fight.

Wilbur continued his chemo throughout the month, and we witnessed more and more lethargy, fatigue, weight gain, and worst of all, apathy.

That is when the true heartbreak began.

Willy, swollen and lethargic

February

I can't bear to write about this month. I wanted to stop this month's chapter 100 percent at "don't want to remember or write about it." Turmoil, choices, decisions, tears, pain, ugly bags under the eyes. But I had to continue. Willy taught me that. Continue to try to fight for Willy while he fought for us. Chemo, sickness, depression. It's all one.

Hank could feel it too, and it was starting to affect his behavior. He hugged Wilbur tightly as much as he could and cuddled him with the blankets in our fluffy, cozy bed. Hank knew it wasn't much longer until he would lose a brother and become an only child again. You could feel his heart breaking.

And each day Wilbur was coming to the office with us; every meeting Wilbur was a part of. He could not be without Aaron or me or he would get upset and make awful sounds. He had his own chair every day at the office or in the conference room.

And he would eat pasta. Only pasta.
I hated this month. All our hearts were being tortured.

Wilbur resting or asleep in a chair at our office

March

This was the most unpleasant month of my life.

The photo below is of Willy's last day at the office. He had come to the office with Aaron and me day after day after day. You can see my eyes welling up, and you can see his swollen enlarged head, sad narrow eyes, and defeat. I forced a smile for him, for the photo.

Holding Willy in my arms at the office for the last time

Willy's final day on this earth with us was so excruciating for Aaron and me. No one could possibly have prepared us for what happened. It was hard enough for us to make the decision to "humanely euthanize" him after many weeks of going back and forth and sleepless nights. We knew that his pain and suffering had gone on too long and he was only keeping himself alive for us. We could not in good conscience force him to continue in agony any longer. Not for us.

On his final day with us, we were told that he would not feel a thing, and the process would be like he was falling asleep.

Please stop reading or prepare yourself for what is coming next, because I have never experienced something like this in my life—not then, and not now, thirteen years later.

While in Aaron's loving arms, Wilbur was injected with what I now call the venom. He was awake, his eyes were open, and there was no peace. I could almost feel the venom going through his feeble little body, cold and tingling. I wanted to scream out at the top of my lungs in agony, *Help!*

Then Willy did what I never could have prepared my heart for. He fought. He resisted the venom hard. Thank God that Aaron could not see his eyes, could not see him struggle to stay alive for us. I watched Willy jerk, and as he stared me down with his eyes bigger than I had seen in some time, I knew that I would never forget that moment in time. It's ingrained for all eternity in my mind and on my heart.

After all that he had been through, Wilbur, Willy, our baby boy, was fighting for one more moment, one more second with us. This was beyond any unconditional love I could imagine.

Each month, each day, each moment we had him close as part of our family was worth all of it.

Willy, you are with us. Each and every day. You are tattooed on our hearts, etched in our minds. There is no forgetting you. You taught me how to be patient, how to love at all costs, how to fight for those I love—and that I would do this again and again.

I am so happy you and Hank are together.

You were *my* nine months, my baby boy I delivered to doggie heaven. My sweet angel, for now until we meet again …

Afterword

Here's something that has always intrigued me. When I was younger, every palm reader at parties or events told me that I would have two boys. Well, I have been blessed with five rescued boys. Most recently, in November 2020, Aaron and I adopted Snoopy and Charlie from Love Bugs Rescue in Southern California. They are brothers from the same "Charlie Brown" litter of five, with sisters Lucy and Sally, and another brother Linus.

They are our babies and our loves. We may not have received the gift of human babies but are so thankful for all the experiences and joy our rescues have brought to us throughout our lives. They have provided us with the opportunity to care for and adore them!

Snoopy and Charlie in Laguna Hills, California

We have Wilbur's ashes in a large decorative wooden box with his favorite yellow blanket, collar, and handwritten and handmade cards from our friends, his vet, and family. We keep the open chest in our bedroom on a stand so all our rescue dogs can feel him with them.

Thank you, Willy, for inspiring us to rescue and adopt you, Flash, Wylie, Snoopy, and Charlie. We will continue to help dogs in need and encourage others to rescue too! Always.

In Loving Memory of Flash

adopted at three years, passed at twelve years

Flash's NVSPCA adoption photo (yes, he was one-eyed and previously named Fluff n Stuff)

Flash and me on Adoption Day outside the Nevada SPCA

Flash in his favorite spot—Aaron's arms

In Loving Memory of Wylie

adopted at three years, passed at ten years

My anxiety-ridden baby boy Wylie, adopted from NVSPCA

Wylie giving me love—his way

Flash and Wylie in St. Croix, US Virgin Islands—loving life!

A Place to Journal Your Own Memories of Loss and Love

Name of loved one lost:
Favorite memory:

Name of loved one lost:
Favorite memory:

Name of loved one lost:
Favorite memory:

Acknowledgments

Special thanks to:

    Mae Morton, for being a part of Wilbur's story and the beautiful handmade cards

    Rebecca Foster, for photos and memories

    Nevada SPCA, for caring for my babies before I met them

    Molly's Mutts, California, for being an awesome rescue and giving me the opportunity to adopt Wilbur

    LoveBugs Rescue, California, for taking in and fostering the Charlie Brown litter

    Every person and family who fosters or adopts rescue dogs

Printed in the USA
CPSIA information can be obtained
at www.ICGtesting.com
JSHW021344291023
50899JS00001B/81